...

Yona Zeldis McDonough

SISTERS IN STRENGTH

American Women Who Made a Difference

ILLUSTRATED BY Malcah Zeldis

...

HENRY HOLT AND COMPANY
NEW YORK

■ ■ ■

In memory of Pamela Askew,
teacher and friend
—Y. Z. M.

For James and Kate,
my beloved grandchildren
—M. Z.

■ ■ ■

I would like to thank my wonderful editor, Christy Ottaviano,
for treating this project as if it were her only one.—Y. Z. M.

Henry Holt and Company, LLC
Publishers since 1866
115 West 18th Street, New York, New York 10011

Henry Holt is a registered trademark of Henry Holt and Company, LLCa
Text copyright © 2000 by Yona Zeldis McDonough
Illustrations copyright © 2000 by Malcah Zeldis. All rights reserved.
Published in Canada by Fitzhenry & Whiteside Ltd.,
195 Allstate Parkway, Markham, Ontario L3R 4T8.

Library of Congress Cataloging-in-Publication Data
McDonough, Yona Zeldis. Sisters in strength: American women who made a difference /
Yona Zeldis McDonough; illustrated by Malcah Zeldis. Includes bibliographical references.
Summary: Profiles eleven women from different times and fields of endeavor whose lives are
meant to serve as role models, including Pocahontas, Harriet Tubman, Elizabeth Cady Stanton,
Susan B. Anthony, Clara Barton, Emily Dickinson, Mary Cassatt, Helen Keller, Eleanor Roosevelt,
Amelia Earhart, and Margaret Mead. 1. Women—United States—Biography—Juvenile literature.
2. Role models—United States—Juvenile literature. [1. Women—Biography.] I. Title.
HQ1412.M25 2000   305.4'092'273—dc21   99-31779
The illustrator used acrylic on illustration board to create the paintings for this book.

ISBN 0-8050-6102-9
First Edition—2000
Printed in the United States of America on acid-free paper. ∞
1 3 5 7 9 10 8 6 4 2

CONTENTS

AUTHOR'S NOTE

Researching and writing about important American women was both a challenge and an inspiration—a challenge because it was difficult to sort through the many impressive lives and select only eleven on which to focus; an inspiration because the stories of those lives are so moving and uplifting.

This book offers a window on different kinds of accomplishment. Amelia Earhart, whose life perhaps best exemplifies one of action—the ultimate exterior life—is a striking contrast to Emily Dickinson, whose secluded yet infinitely rich life is the perfect embodiment of an interior one. The lives of Harriet Tubman and Clara Barton teach lessons about service to others and respect for the basic human condition. The stories of these women, and all the others included, contain their own essential set of values and wisdom.

Leadership, humanitarianism, dignity, creativity—these are just some of the qualities the women in these stories possess. And it is my hope that these qualities will seem worthy of emulation by young readers.

—*Yona Zeldis McDonough*

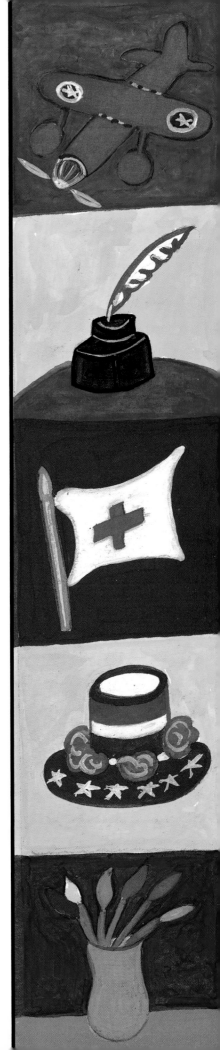

5

POCAHONTAS

c. 1595–1617

[She had a] compassionate pitifull (sympathetic) heart [that]
gave me much cause to respect her.

—Captain John Smith, writing of Pocahontas in his book
Generall Historie of Virginia, New-England, and the Summer Isles (1624)

Although Powhatan had many children by different wives, his favorite daughter was the young Pocahontas. Powhatan was the Algonkian people's chief, a powerful tribal leader who lived in what is now the state of Virginia; Pocahontas was his princess.

No one knows very much about her early years. Like most of Powhatan's children, Pocahontas was taken away from her mother at birth and raised in her father's household. The ordinary chores that Algonkian girls performed—gardening, fetching water, gathering wood, sewing deerskins, preparing and cooking food—would not have been expected of her. Instead, she probably spent her days swimming and playing in the woods. Although her real name was Matoaka, her nickname of Pocahontas, which means "playful one," suited her better.

Pocahontas was about twelve when she first met the English settlers who landed on the shores of the Chesapeake Bay. The English had come seeking more space for their own people and new markets for their woolen coats and blankets. They also believed the new world had gold, which they wanted to bring home. In 1607 they established Jamestown, a settlement named after King James I. It had a trading post, a church, a storehouse, and a group of thatched houses. Clearly, the English intended to stay.

Powhatan viewed the settlers with suspicion. He liked their

glass beads and copper kettle he had bartered for with bushels of corn. And he longed for their guns. But he feared that the English would attack his people and steal his land. Pocahontas, however, was intrigued by the foreigners and was a frequent visitor to Jamestown. It was there that she met Captain John Smith, and the two became friends.

Pocahontas taught Smith to speak her language, and Smith taught her English. She loved to watch as the colonists built their homes and cleared land for fields. She began to care for these odd but endearing strangers. When their food supply grew low, Pocahontas urged her people to come to Jamestown with more. She told Smith about other tribes willing to trade food. He later said that Pocahontas was "the instrument [that saved] this colony from death, famine, and utter confusion." She also saved Smith. When she learned of her father's plans to kill him, she sneaked into the settlement to warn him, and Smith was able to make his escape.

Despite Pocahontas's efforts to promote peace between the English and the Algonkians, tensions grew between the two groups. When her father ordered the massacre of sixty colonists, Pocahontas left to live with the Potomac tribe up north. Soon after this, the Potomacs received a visit from an Englishman, Samuel Argall, a captain who had lost his way while trying to reach Bermuda. Pocahontas was glad to meet him, not knowing that he was scheming to kidnap and hold her for ransom. With the help of two Potomac friends he had bribed, Argall lured Pocahontas to visit his ship. He served her dinner, and afterward the Potomacs quietly sailed away, leaving her in the hands of the English.

Pocahontas was taken to the farm of a minister, where her short doeskin skirt was replaced by a tight, fitted corset, long-sleeved blouse, and heavy long skirt. She was instructed in Christianity and baptized a Christian under the name of Rebecca. But Argall's plan failed: Powhatan was unwilling to negotiate for Pocahontas's release, and she surprisingly came to like her captors, who treated her well.

When tobacco grower John Rolfe asked her to marry him, she agreed. Although Powhatan didn't attend the ceremony, his views on the English must have softened, for he gave Pocahontas a pearl necklace and a large parcel of land as wedding gifts.

The next year, Pocahontas gave birth to a baby boy whom she named Thomas. When he was about a year old, the little family set sail for England. Pocahontas was dazzled by the wonders of London, and was even invited to Whitehall Palace where she met Queen Anne. But she was not used to the damp English weather and she became ill, coughing and growing weaker by the day. Still, when the ship was ready to set sail for home, she got on board. But before they reached the Atlantic Ocean, Pocahontas knew she would not survive the journey. She begged her husband to bring her ashore, so the ship dropped anchor, and she was brought to a nearby inn, where she died.

The young woman who had worked so hard to bring peace in her native land died and was buried at Gravesend on English soil.

HARRIET TUBMAN

c. 1820–1913

*I looked at my hands to see if I was the same person now that
I was free. There was such a glory over everything.
The sun came like gold through the trees and over the fields,
and I felt like I was in heaven.*

—Harriet Tubman, describing her arrival in Pennsylvania

Mrs. Cook showed Minty yet again how to wind the yarn into balls. It was hard work, and if Minty did it wrong, the white woman whipped her.

Minty, whose given name was Araminta, was born a slave in Maryland, the daughter of Harriet Greene and Benjamin Ross, both slaves. At an early age, she had been hired out to the Cooks by Mr. Brodas, who owned her and her family. Although she was only six, she had to work all day. At night, she slept by the fire, burying her feet in the ashes to keep them warm.

The Cooks were not happy with her, and when Minty got sick they sent her home. Next, Mr. Brodas hired Minty out to Miss Susan, to watch her baby. When the baby cried at night and woke the mistress, Minty was whipped. Later, Minty stole a lump of sugar from the table and rather than face a beating from Miss Susan, she hid in a pigpen. When she finally came out, Mr. Brodas did not hire her out again, but instead let her work in the fields.

The field slaves talked as they worked. They spoke of freedom and escape. Minty heard about the Underground Railroad, a network of people who led slaves to freedom. She also heard talk of Nat Turner, a black preacher who started a rebellion to end slavery. He was caught and killed, but his story gave Minty ideas. Once, she defied the overseer—the man in charge of keeping the slaves in

11

line—and helped another slave escape. The furious overseer threw a heavy metal weight at the slave who was fleeing. It hit Minty instead. She nearly died from a fractured skull. When she recovered, she had a scar that marked her for life. People respected her courage. They no longer used her nickname, Minty, but started calling her by the name she chose—Harriet—her mother's name.

When Harriet was about twenty-three, she fell in love with and married John Tubman, a free black man. She sewed a beautiful patchwork quilt for their bed and moved to his cabin. John was happy, but Harriet worried. Her old master, Mr. Brodas, had died, and she was now owned by Dr. Anthony Thompson. What if he sold her? She begged John to flee north, but he refused.

Harriet's fears came true. Dr. Thompson had sold her and three of her brothers. A slave trader would soon be coming for all of them. Harriet knew the men wouldn't have time to escape, so she went alone. Packing a little food and the quilt, she set off into the woods after everyone was asleep. The woods were dark and quiet. Harriet waded through streams whenever possible so bloodhounds couldn't follow her scent in the water. She first went to the cabin of a Quaker woman who had become her friend. (The Quakers are a religious group whose main beliefs include opposition to violence and equality for all people.) The woman told her where to stop on her journey. Harriet wanted to thank the woman but had no money, so she gave her the quilt.

Harriet hid by day, sheltered by Quakers, and traveled at night. Finally, she reached Philadelphia, Pennsylvania, where she was now free. Free! Harriet was happy, but also sad—everyone she loved was far away. She made a vow to go back to see her family, and when she did, she would bring them north.

In time, Harriet found a job in a hotel. Soon she met abolitionists (people who believed slavery was wrong and worked to end it) and "conductors" on the Underground Railroad that stretched from the South to Canada where slaves became free. Then Harriet learned that her sister and her family were about to be sold. Despite the danger, she went to Maryland and brought her sister's family safely north. It was her first time as a conductor on the Underground Railroad. It was not her last.

For seven years, she traveled back and forth, bringing slaves up north. One time, dressed as a man to fool the slave owners, she went back for her husband, John. She was crushed to find he had taken another wife and would not come along with her. Her most memorable trip was in June 1857 when she hired a wagon and brought her aged parents north to freedom.

Harriet grew famous. Slave owners posted a forty-thousand-dollar reward for her capture, dead or alive. Still, she kept making her trips. Friends eventually convinced her to stop traveling so she began to give talks about her adventures. Around that time she bought a small farm near Auburn, New York, her home for the rest of her life. When the Civil War broke out in 1861, Harriet began to help former slaves adjust to their new lives; she became a nurse, a cook, and a spy.

Four years later when the war ended, she returned home to Auburn, New York. There, she cared for her parents. Poor ex-slaves came to her for help. Harriet set up a nursing home and a hospital for them—the Harriet Tubman Home for Indigent Aged Negroes. When she died at the age of ninety-two, people mourned the woman who had earned the name of Moses, because she had brought so many of her people out of slavery.

ELIZABETH CADY STANTON
1815–1902

SUSAN B. ANTHONY
1820–1906

We hold these truths to be self-evident:
that all men and women are created equal.

—Opening words of the Declaration of Sentiments and Resolutions,
written by Elizabeth Cady Stanton

Tall, slender, and single, Susan B. Anthony seemed to have little in common with Elizabeth Cady Stanton, a tiny, plump mother of three. Yet years later Elizabeth wrote, "I liked her thoroughly from the beginning." Their long friendship was devoted to the same goal: obtaining basic rights for the women of America.

Elizabeth, one of Judge Cady's four daughters, grew up in Johnstown, New York. Her brother, Eleazar, was their father's favorite. Judge Cady hoped his son would become a judge, but Eleazar died young. While the judge sat grieving, Elizabeth climbed on his lap to comfort him. He said, "Oh, my daughter, I wish you were a boy!"

Most people preferred boys to girls; Elizabeth knew that. Maybe she could be the kind of girl who was just as good as a boy. She asked the retired Presbyterian minister next door to teach her Greek—something usually taught only to boys—and she learned to ride a horse. She also enrolled in the Johnstown Academy (which, unlike most high schools of that time, admitted girls) and studied hard.

Because colleges did not accept women, Elizabeth could not attend. But she enrolled in the Troy Female Seminary. Her father hoped she would soon marry. Instead, she spent time in Peterboro, New Hampshire, with her mother's cousin, Gerrit Smith, an aboli-

tionist who sheltered runaway slaves. Through Smith, she met Henry Brewster Stanton, who delivered stirring antislavery speeches. Henry and Elizabeth fell in love, and married. They became involved in the abolitionist cause. But Elizabeth was angered to find that many abolitionists felt only men should represent the cause at conventions. She and a new friend, Lucretia Mott, decided to hold a convention of their own. They would debate another burning question—that of equal rights for women.

It took them eight years to accomplish this goal. During those years, Elizabeth was busy raising her three boys virtually alone in Seneca Falls, New York, while her husband traveled. She now understood what most women endured: endless chores with little or no help from their husbands.

The first Women's Rights Convention took place on July 19, 1848. Three hundred people gathered to hear the arguments. Elizabeth gave the first speech, which shocked many people who thought it wasn't ladylike for a woman to address a crowd. She was followed by others who spoke out for freedom and equality. Elizabeth was tired but happy; history was being made that night. By this time, too, she asked her friends to address their letters to Elizabeth Cady Stanton, rather than to Mrs. Henry Stanton. She felt that a woman should not lose her identity just because she was married.

Meanwhile, in Rochester, New York, another determined young woman had heard about the convention. Her name was Susan Brownell Anthony. Born in Adams, Massachusetts, Susan was the daughter of Quakers. Her father, Daniel Anthony, was an abolitionist, and Susan often took part in heated conversations about subjects such as slavery.

Susan's father had a small cotton mill. When one of the workers was unable to work for two weeks, Susan took her place and was paid wages. Although many people criticized her father, Susan was proud to earn money.

But Susan wasn't destined to be a mill worker. Instead, she continued her education at a female Quaker seminary in Philadelphia, though it was cut short when her father's business failed and she returned home to help. She became a teacher, first in New Rochelle, New York, and later near Rochester, New York, where she enjoyed her work even though she thought it unfair to be paid roughly one quarter of what a man would have earned doing the same job. When she heard about the Seneca Falls convention and Elizabeth Cady Stanton, Susan knew she had to meet her.

Susan and Elizabeth became a team. Elizabeth, now the mother of six, found traveling hard, so she wrote the speeches that Susan delivered. Together, they set out to win property rights for married women, who under the laws at that time were not allowed to own property themselves. It took years, but in 1860 New York State passed a law allowing married women control over money they earned and anything they inherited. This was only the start. Now Susan and Elizabeth were determined to secure for women the right to vote. But many people believed that women didn't deserve to vote. Changing people's minds was not going to be easy.

The two women launched a speaking tour and gathered thousands of signatures on petitions. Elizabeth wrote pamphlets that Susan sold to raise money. They started a newspaper, *The Revolution*, and published books on the history of the women's rights movement.

When Elizabeth died in 1902, Susan said, "How lonesome I do feel!" And when she herself died four years later, only Wyoming, Utah, Colorado, and Idaho had given women the right to vote. Finally in 1920, the United States passed an amendment to the Constitution granting all women the right to go to the ballot box. Without the work of Susan and Elizabeth, it would not have happened.

17

CLARA BARTON

1821–1912

The wounded were brought to me, frozen, for days after. . . .
The many wounded lay, uncared for, on the cold snow.

—Clara Barton, describing the Battle of Fredricksburg

On Christmas day in 1821, a baby girl was born in North Oxford, Massachusetts. Her name—Clarissa Harlowe Barton—seemed too fancy for every day, so she was called Clara. Clara was much younger than her sisters and brothers. They doted on her and taught her many things: reading, writing, math, horseback riding, and carpentry. Her mother was strict but warm hearted; instead of giving Clara toys or dolls, she taught her to cook, sew, and run a house.

Clara was bright but very shy. At the age of eleven, she spent much of her time nursing and being a companion to her brother during an illness. This experience would help her greatly in the future. Her mother was told that Clara needed more responsibility and that becoming a schoolteacher would be good for her, so at eighteen, Clara took over a one-room schoolhouse. Some of the older boys were bullies, who had made their previous teacher's life miserable. On her first day, Clara asked to join their games at recess. They were astonished to see how fast she ran and how well she threw a ball. There was no problem with those boys—or any of the other students—after that.

Clara gained a reputation for being able to handle difficult children. She spent ten years setting one troubled school in order and

19

moving on to the next. Then in 1850, she improved upon her own education by attending a teachers' school in Clinton, New York, for a year, after which she returned to teaching in New Jersey. A few years later while visiting nearby Bordentown, New Jersey, she was disturbed to learn that there were no "free" (or public) schools, as there were in Massachusetts. Parents paid for children to attend school, and if they couldn't afford it the children couldn't go. Clara made an offer to the school committee—if given a school, she would teach without pay.

The next day, Clara had her school. It was a run-down old building and on the first day of classes, only six students showed up. But two years later, the school had six hundred pupils and was housed in a brand-new building. The committee decided it shouldn't be run by a woman and hired a male principal. Clara was so angry that she left the position and the teaching profession. She got a job in the Post Office Department in Washington, D.C., and was perhaps the first appointed civil servant.

Not long after Abraham Lincoln was elected president and the Civil War began, Clara, working in Washington, D.C., worried about the soldiers she saw pouring in from the battlefields—wounded, bleeding, and without their baggage. She placed an ad in the newspaper asking for donations of food, bandages, medicine, and clothing. Soon she had no place to keep all the materials she received. She wanted to deliver supplies where they were most needed: the battlefield.

The War Department was shocked. Women couldn't visit the battlefield! But she kept asking and finally was given a pass for herself and three volunteers. Miraculously, she also received carts and teams of mules for carrying supplies. At the front, Clara served soup from laundry tubs, ladled out gallons of hot coffee, and oversaw the baking of hundreds of loaves of bread.

Clara knew that the wounded men might not survive the long trip to a hospital, so she began treating them on the battlefield—a radical new idea. In nursing stations set up in tents and wagons, Clara tended the sick. She insisted upon also treating Confederate soldiers from the enemy's army, although this too shocked the War Department. The men called Clara the "Angel of the Battlefield."

After the Civil War ended in 1865, Clara Barton used her own money to set up an organization to trace missing soldiers and to identify the bodies of the dead. The hard work made her weary and weak, so in 1869 she went to Switzerland to rest.

In Geneva she learned about the International Committee of the Red Cross, an organization that helped sick and wounded soldiers in wartime. Clara returned to America and urged President Rutherford B. Hayes to join. He said no. Because many Americans wished to believe there would never be war in America again, Clara stressed a peacetime mission for the Red Cross: helping victims of floods, fires, earthquakes, droughts, hurricanes, and epidemics.

In 1881, Clara Barton with the help of others established the American Association of the Red Cross. She was named its first president. Years later when she was in her sixties, Clara went to Johnstown, Pennsylvania, five days after a terrible flood had ravaged the city. She stayed for five months, living and working in a tent, with an empty box for a desk. During the Spanish-American War, Clara rode onto the battlefield in a wagon to feed and nurse the sick, and she set up orphanages for Cuban children whose parents had disappeared or been killed.

When Clara died at the age of ninety-one, her body was taken from Glen Echo, Maryland, where she had been living, back to North Oxford, Massachusetts, for burial. The carriage driver responsible for the coffin told how Clara Barton had saved his father, a Confederate soldier, whom she found bleeding to death on the battlefield. Now it was the son's turn to repay that kindness, and bring this dedicated soul home to rest.

EMILY DICKINSON
1830–1886

If I read a book [and] it makes my whole body so cold no fire
can ever warm me, I know that is poetry. If I feel physically
as if the top of my head were taken off, I know that is poetry.

—Emily Dickinson, in a conversation with Thomas Wentworth Higginson

Emily was a shy girl; still, she was invited to fudge-making parties, sleigh rides, picnics, and maple-sugar parties in her hometown of Amherst, Massachusetts. She liked her books and her dictionary (calling them her "strongest friends") and was allowed to have a good education for a girl of her time. She attended Amherst Academy off and on for six years, and later, the nearby Mount Holyoke Female Seminary. Emily didn't like the seminary, where the girls were made to stand up and proclaim their religious faith in public, and she was relieved to return home after only a year.

The death of her girlhood friend, Sophia Holland, was a great blow to Emily, and she gradually began to withdraw from the world. Although she visited Washington, D.C., where her father was a member of Congress, and Philadelphia in her twenties, and later went to Boston to have her eyes examined, she grew more reclusive.

Eventually Emily would not leave the grounds of the house where she had grown up. She gradually refused to see visitors, who were forced to talk with her through the closed door to her room. Once, she lowered a basket filled with warm gingerbread for the children who were playing beneath her window. Giggling, they took it. After that, they tried to catch glimpses of her through the

23

tall hedges, but rarely did they spot her. If they did, she was always in white, for as time went by, she stopped wearing any other color. In fact, Emily would not let the seamstress who made her clothes see her; instead, her clothes were fitted on her sister, Lavinia, who also lived at home and to whom she remained close.

But Emily lived a rich and productive life inside her own mind. Throughout the day, as she did her chores—baking bread, tending the garden, frying doughnuts—she wrote poems in newspaper margins or on scraps of paper. Later, alone in her room, she would copy the poem neatly in ink. She bound several of these poems together with thread and tucked the booklet in a locked box that she kept hidden in her cherry-wood dresser.

Her poems were unconventional, startling, and brilliant. Nature, love, death, and God were subjects she returned to often, and she noted the details of the natural world with a sharp, observant eye. Emily's poems tended to be short and in them she boldly experimented with rhythm—often using a songlike structure—as well as with rhyme and punctuation. Here is one of her poems about a cat:

> She sights a Bird—she chuckles—
> She flattens—then she crawls—
> She runs without the look of feet—
> Her eyes increase to Balls—
>
> Her Jaws stir—twitching—hungry—
> Her Teeth can hardly stand—
> She leaps, but Robin leaped the first—
> Ah, Pussy, of the Sand,
>
> The Hopes so juicy ripening—
> You almost bathed your Tongue—
> When Bliss disclosed a hundred Toes—
> And fled with every one.

Life was quiet but fruitful in Amherst, filled with chores and letter writing. In her letters, which still exist, Emily emerges as charming, witty, and very much the "quaint, old fashioned friend" that she called herself. Emily also took long walks with her dog, Carlo. When her mother was ill, she cared for her patiently. And always, there was her poetry.

Emily rarely let anyone see her poems; her stern, distant father never read a single one. Thomas Wentworth Higginson, a well-known writer and critic with whom she corresponded, saw a few. Higginson discouraged Emily from seeking the publication of her work. At the time, he did not seem to have understood her immense gift, though later he may have changed his mind. In any case, Emily must have listened to his advice because only seven poems were published in her lifetime.

When Emily died, Lavinia found almost 1,800 poems tied up in neat little packets in Emily's bureau. She was startled by the sheer number of them and recognized the genius they represented. Lavinia devoted herself to getting the work published and read. It is largely because of her dedication and effort that Emily Dickinson is now regarded as one of America's greatest and most original poets.

MARY CASSATT

1844–1926

I used to go and flatten my nose against that window and
absorb all I could of his art. It changed my life.
I saw art then as I wanted to see it.

—Mary Cassatt, writing about the art of Edgar Degas

Seven-year-old Mary stood rapt as she watched the artist dip his
brush into the paint. He had been hired to do a portrait of her three
brothers, Alexander, Gardner, and Robbie. Mary wouldn't have
minded joining them to pose. But even more exciting was watching
the way the artist worked, and how from indistinct dabs of paint on
the canvas, he created a convincing image of his subjects. It was the
first time Mary had seen an artist at work, and although she did not
know it, her life had already been set on its course.

One of five children, Mary lived in the town of Allegheny City,
Pennsylvania. Shortly after the portrait of her brothers was completed,
her family moved to Paris, France, where she was able to visit great
museums, like the Louvre. Then they moved to Germany, but after
Robbie got sick and died, the grief-stricken family returned home.

At sixteen Mary was taking classes at the Pennsylvania Academy
of Fine Arts, where she learned how to draw the human body. But
she wanted to go back to Europe, to study the paintings of Leonardo
da Vinci, Rembrandt, and Titian. Mary yearned to become a pro-
fessional artist, not an amateur. This was a radical idea, and when
her father heard it, he said, "I would almost rather see you dead!"
But eventually, Mary persuaded him to let her go, accompanied by
her mother.

In Paris, Mary studied with established painters and was thrilled when one of her paintings, *A Mandolin Player*, was accepted to the Paris Salon for its 1868 exhibition. Soon, more of her paintings were accepted by the Salon. (Since the seventeenth century it had been the goal of young painters to be accepted by the Salon, the annual or biennial official French exhibition of painting and sculpture.)

Then Mary discovered the work of the French artist Edgar Degas, and the direction of her artistic life changed dramatically. The two met and formed a friendship that would last forty years. With Degas as her inspiration, Mary began to experiment with a bolder, flatter form of design, and with brighter, lighter colors. She stopped showing her work in the Salon and began to exhibit paintings with a group of modern artists known as the Impressionists. Their broad, sketchy brush strokes and light-infused canvases were ridiculed by critics.

One of the things the critics particularly scorned was the Impressionists' choice of subject matter. Instead of painting scenes from history or mythology, these artists painted scenes of everyday life. Mary started with pictures of her sister at her loom and a young woman at the theater. Then she painted a mother giving a little girl a bath; a child stroking her mother's face; a woman seated in a rowboat with a plump baby resting in her lap. Her portraits were not commissioned; instead, she used family and friends as her subjects. Yet despite the tender feelings for children expressed in her paintings, she never had any of her own. "A woman artist must be . . . capable of making the primary sacrifices," she told an interviewer. Perhaps she was speaking of how difficult it would be to raise a family and maintain her life as an artist.

In time, Mary became very famous and her work was well known in artistic circles. She was asked to paint a twelve-by-fifty-eight-foot mural for the Women's Building of the Chicago World's Columbian Exposition. Even her father was impressed and said, "She is now known to the Art world as well as to the general public in such a way as not to be forgotten again so long as she continues to paint!" She was able to buy a large summer house outside Paris, where she painted, tended her many rosebushes, and entertained her family and friends.

Although she spent much of her adult life in Europe, Mary always considered herself "definitely and frankly" an American, and she was troubled by the scarcity of good paintings that were available for viewing in her native country. She helped her family and American friends build art collections that would eventually go to museums, since she wanted young artists to be inspired in the way she had.

Mary lived to be eighty-two, and kept working in oil paints, pastels, and prints until failing eyesight made her stop. When that happened, she worked to support other causes, like the campaign for women's rights that was going on in America. Shortly before her death she wrote, "I have not done what I wanted but I tried to make a good fight." Many think it was a fight that she won.

HELEN KELLER

1880–1968

I will always—as long as I have breath—work for the handicapped.

—Helen Keller, to a reporter on her eightieth birthday

Captain Keller and his wife watched as their baby Helen twisted and moaned with fever. Doctors were unable to help, and the Kellers feared she would die. Miraculously, Helen recovered. But she could no longer see or hear, and was condemned to a silent, dark world.

Her early life in Tuscumbia, Alabama, was hard. Although bright, Helen was always frustrated by her condition. She fell or slammed into things when she played or ran. Other children avoided her because she hit them or broke their toys. When she smelled the cake her mother had baked for her sixth birthday, she destroyed it with her hands and stuffed chunks of it into her mouth. Her mother wanted to save the cake for a special supper, so she took it away, but Helen began to sob and kick. When her mother tried to comfort her, Helen rushed outside, right into a thorny bush. The birthday supper was ruined. At that point, the Kellers knew they had to find someone to help their daughter.

Not long after this realization, the Kellers traveled to Washington, D.C., where Helen met Alexander Graham Bell, the inventor of the telephone. Dr. Bell had spent years trying to help deaf people. He took Helen on his lap. She touched his beard and held his pocket watch to her cheek to feel its ticking. Dr. Bell told her parents about

31

a special school for the blind in Boston, where a blind and deaf girl had been taught to communicate. Maybe the school would send a teacher for the Kellers.

Helen was soon startled by the arrival of a young stranger, Anne Sullivan. Anne had been nearly blind before an operation restored her sight. Now she was here to help Helen. She gave Helen a doll and then took her hand and pressed strange and unfamiliar patterns on it with her fingers. Anne was making the letters D-O-L-L. Helen was confused, but soon learned to imitate the patterns. C-A-T was for when they stroked the cat. C-A-K-E meant she wanted a treat and M-I-L-K a drink. But Helen didn't understand that she was spelling words.

Life with "Miss Annie" was a roller-coaster ride. Helen liked the sewing cards and beads Miss Annie gave her, as well as their walks and pony rides in the woods. But Miss Annie was strict. No more roaming around the table, grabbing food. Helen had to sit in her chair, fold her napkin, and eat with a spoon. The rules made Helen angry. She would hit Miss Annie. Helen even locked the teacher in a room and hid the key.

Then one day, they stopped beside the outdoor pump. Helen held her hand under the spout while Annie pumped. Annie took her other hand and spelled W-A-T-E-R. All at once, something in Helen's face changed. She spelled water herself, several times. She pointed down, and Annie spelled out G-R-O-U-N-D. Suddenly, Helen understood that the signs she had been making were words, and words could be attached to objects, people, animals—anything at all! She pointed to Annie, and Annie spelled T-E-A-C-H-E-R, which became her new name. That night Helen kissed Annie for the very first time.

Next, Annie taught Helen braille, which is a way for blind people to read by running their fingers over a series of letters printed in raised dots. As Helen learned more, her temper improved. Soon she was able to dress herself, make her bed, and pick up her toys. Helen even learned to speak, slowly and painstakingly, by placing her fingers on the lips of someone speaking, and then copying the shapes and movements that person's mouth made to create sounds.

Helen became a model student, first, at the Wright-Humason School in New York City and, later, at the Cambridge School for Young Ladies. She was eventually accepted to Radcliffe College in 1900. When classes began, Annie was right by her side, spelling what the professors said into Helen's hand. English was her best subject. Some of the things she wrote were published, and a magazine offered her money to write the story of her life. After Helen graduated from Radcliffe in 1904, she and Annie went to live in Wrentham, near Boston. Annie married John Macy, one of Helen's former teachers at Radcliffe, and he came to live with them.

Helen began to lecture on the needs of the blind and deaf. Because of her, many organizations to educate blind and deaf people were created. One of her goals was to get more books printed in braille. The National Library for the Blind was established in part due to her efforts.

When the American Foundation for the Blind was started, Helen went to work there. Then Helen's mother died, and soon after, Annie did, too. Helen mourned them both.

Still, her work went on. After America entered the Second World War in 1941, President Franklin Roosevelt asked her to visit soldiers who had been blinded in the fighting. She was proud of the Helen Keller World Crusade, started by the United Nations. Now there would be help for blind and deaf children in so many countries. When Helen Keller died in 1968, her message of dignity and education had been heard and heeded all over the world.

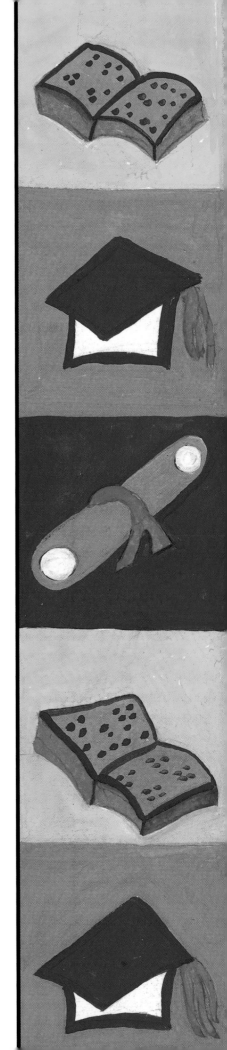

ELEANOR ROOSEVELT
1884–1962

Where, after all, do universal rights begin? In small places, close
to home ... in the world of the individual person ... where every man,
woman, and child seeks equal justice, equal opportunity, and
equal dignity, without discrimination.

—Eleanor Roosevelt, in a speech given at the United Nations

Granny. That's what Eleanor's beautiful, elegant mother called her,
because she was so shy and serious. Mother often seemed disap-
pointed with her. She told Eleanor, "You have no looks, so see to it
that you have manners." Eleanor felt more comfortable with her
good-natured father. But sometimes Father's behavior was odd.
Only years later did Eleanor learn that her father was an alcoholic.
Drinking liquor made him say and do peculiar things. By the time
she was ten, both her parents and her younger brother were dead.

Eleanor and her older brother were raised by Grandmother
Hall. Although she tried hard to please her aloof grandmother,
Eleanor felt the older woman wasn't interested in her. She was
relieved when she was sent to Allenswood, a school for girls in
England. The time spent in England was happy; Mademoiselle
Souvestre, the school's director, understood and encouraged her.
Eleanor made many friends and when she returned to America, she
did so with a newfound confidence.

Eleanor had inherited enough money so that she would never
have to work. Still, she wanted to be useful, so she volunteered as a
teacher in a poor New York neighborhood. One of her distant
cousins, Franklin, heard about what she was doing. He was eager to

learn more about her, and after the two had gotten to know each other, he asked her to marry him.

Married life was busy. With six children born in ten years (one child died as a baby) Eleanor always had work to do, either caring for them or assisting in her husband's busy career. First, Franklin went to law school and began his political life as a state senator from New York. Then, President Woodrow Wilson appointed him Assistant Secretary of the Navy, and the Roosevelts moved to Washington, D.C.

In Washington a new life opened up for Eleanor. During World War I, she became the director for a Red Cross center that served thousands of soldiers food and drink. When the war was over, she wrote reports for the League of Women Voters about laws affecting women. Then in 1921, her husband contracted polio, a disease that crippled him. Eleanor helped Franklin get better, although he would wear metal braces on his legs for the rest of his life. She encouraged his political ambitions, bravely going against her mother-in-law who thought Franklin should give up politics and spend his time at home.

So that people would remember him, Eleanor began making speeches for her husband at gatherings of women voters. Her efforts paid off: Franklin was elected governor of New York. Eleanor quickly became Franklin's "legs" and visited prisons and mental hospitals so that she could report on their conditions to him. In addition, she was part owner of a girls' school, where she taught several days a week. When Franklin was elected president in 1932, Eleanor felt sad that she would have to give up her useful life. But she took her many gifts—energy, intelligence, moral purpose, and kindness—with her to the capital, where she became a brand-new kind of first lady.

Always a crusader, Eleanor helped her husband by traveling thousands of miles to inspect government projects, on which she would then report to him. She championed the rights of the poor, the disadvantaged, and the oppressed. The concerns of women, blacks, Jewish refugees, tenant farmers, and textile workers were her concerns, too. She made speeches, drew attention to their different situations, and worked hard on their behalf. In her daily newspaper columns and her radio broadcasts, she reached out to all Americans.

Once when she attended a conference in the racially segregated South, she was told that blacks and whites could not sit together. Eleanor got up from her seat and joined the blacks. A police officer told her that she was breaking the law, so she had a chair placed in the center of the aisle, and there she sat.

After Franklin Roosevelt died, Eleanor continued her work. President Harry Truman encouraged her to become a delegate to the United Nations. It was largely because of her that the United Nations adopted the Universal Declaration of Human Rights. Even after she retired from the United Nations in 1953, Eleanor kept speaking and traveling to promote the cause of world peace. President John F. Kennedy appointed her as a member of the National Advisory Committee of the Peace Corps, and asked her to chair the President's Commission on the Status of Women. Eleanor also received many awards for her humanitarian efforts. "She would rather light a candle than curse the darkness," praised one of her many supporters when she died, "and her glow had warmed the world."

AMELIA EARHART

1897–1937

> Women must try to do things as men have tried.
> When they fail, their failure must be but a challenge to others.

—Amelia Earhart, writing to her husband before her
last round-the-world flight

In the early 1900s, girls weren't supposed to run, jump fences, or play wild games. But that didn't stop Amelia Mary Earhart. Meelie, as she was called, was a tomboy. She never played with dolls; instead she preferred the sports and games that boys played. Even when she read, she liked adventure stories in which boys did exciting things; she wondered why the girls in the stories never had as much fun, although she and her little sister, Muriel, had plenty of fun. Their parents, Amy and Edwin, were loving and gave them lots of room to grow. Once, Meelie and her cousins built a roller coaster in the backyard of her grandparents' house. Meelie was the first passenger.

As she got older, Amelia did well in school. After graduation, she was unsure about what to do next. In 1917 she went to Toronto to spend Christmas with Muriel, who was attending school there. Although the United States had entered World War I only that spring, Canada had been involved since 1914. Amelia was struck by the wounded men she saw, casualties of war, and volunteered as a nurse's aide in a veterans' hospital. She thought she might go into medicine. But when her parents, now living in Los Angeles, asked her to come help them work out personal problems they had been having, she went.

It was in California that flying first caught Amelia's eye. Many

wartime pilots were now trying to earn a living in the air. They gave lessons and performed stunts. When her father arranged a trial flight, Amelia signed up for lessons and took a job in the mailroom of a telephone company to pay for them.

Before long, Amelia got her pilot's license and flew as often as she could. She even began dressing like a flier, in boots, khaki pants, leather jacket, helmet, and goggles. By 1921 she had bought her own plane.

But flying was still largely a man's world. A wealthy woman named Amy Phipps Guest wanted to change that. Inspired by the daring flight of Charles Lindbergh, who in 1927 made the first non-stop solo flight across the Atlantic, Mrs. Guest planned a similar trip herself. When her family persuaded her against it, she asked Amelia to take her place.

As captain, Amelia made all the decisions, but since she lacked the necessary experience, the actual flying was done by pilot Bill Stultz. On June 17, 1928, Amelia, Bill, and mechanic Lou Gordon, took off from Newfoundland in the *Friendship*. After twenty hours and forty minutes, they arrived safely in Wales. Their accomplishment was met with much fanfare. Still, Amelia was bothered that the real heroes—Bill and Lou—were in the shadows while all the attention centered on her. She promised herself that one day she would fly the Atlantic solo.

After the *Friendship* flight, Amelia—or AE, as she was now called—wrote and lectured about flying, competed in the Women's Air Derby, and helped start a new airline. But she longed to fly. In 1931 she married George Putnam, a publisher. She confided in him her dream of flying across the Atlantic alone, and he encouraged her.

AE began preparing. Her Lockheed Vega needed alterations before she could take it over the ocean, so she practiced "flying blind" until she knew she could handle the plane on instruments alone. Finally, on May 21, 1932, she took off from Harbour Grace, Newfoundland, on her historic solo flight.

At first, the flight went smoothly, but soon mechanical difficulties arose. When her instruments malfunctioned, she was forced to fly through fog and darkness without knowing her distance from the ocean. AE ran into a storm and was pelted by rain and wind. More parts of the Lockheed Vega failed. But she kept steady on her course and brought the plane safely down in Ireland. AE had made it across the Atlantic in slightly less than fifteen hours! Fame and fortune quickly followed, and she and George went to London, Paris, and Rome, with AE meeting royalty and foreign dignitaries in each city. Back home, she was invited to the White House to meet President Herbert Hoover.

When in 1935 she got a new plane, the twin-engine Lockheed Electra, AE decided to try what was then aviation's greatest challenge: a flight around the world along the equator. It had been done, but never by a woman, and always just north of the equator.

Amelia and George prepared for months. They studied maps and weather patterns, and AE chose a flight partner, Fred Noonan, a commercial pilot and navigator. There was one false start, which delayed the flight, but finally, on June 1, 1937, all was ready. AE and Noonan climbed into the Electra and took off. During the longest and most dangerous part of the trip—a 2,556-mile stretch from New Guinea to a tiny mid-Pacific spot called Howland Island—the plane was lost. Earhart and Noonan disappeared. No trace of their bodies or the plane was ever found.

People have continued to wonder what happened. Did her plane run out of fuel and sink into the ocean? We may never know. But the words she wrote to her father many years earlier, before her flight on the *Friendship*, serve as her epitaph: "Hooray for the last grand adventure! I wish I had won, but it was worthwhile anyway."

41

MARGARET MEAD
1901–1978

I must admit I personally measure success in terms of the contributions an individual makes to her or his fellow human beings.

—Margaret Mead, in *Redbook* magazine

It was Grandma Mead who first encouraged Margaret to think like an anthropologist. She told her to take notes on the behavior of her two younger sisters, Elizabeth and Priscilla. Margaret jotted down many things her sisters said and did. In some ways they were quite different from each other, while in others they were quite similar. She didn't know that she had already begun her life as an anthropologist—someone who studies the physical, social, and cultural lives of human beings—and that her very first field trip was right in her own backyard.

Margaret was the eldest of five children. For the first few years of their lives, they were taught at home by their mother and grandmother. Grandma Mead didn't think children should have to sit still for more than an hour, and she disapproved of their memorizing lists of facts. Instead, she sent Margaret outdoors to bring her examples of a plant she had described in a lesson. Margaret's mother felt that children needed to use their hands, so she had her children learn carpentry, basket making, weaving, and carving. Because Margaret's father worked as a professor, the family moved many times when she was a child. By the time she was a teenager, the Meads had lived in sixty different houses! The ability to feel at home in a

new place was a quality Margaret prized highly, particularly as she grew older.

After graduating from Barnard College and earning a doctorate in anthropology at Columbia University in New York City, Margaret traveled nine thousand miles to American Samoa, an island east of Australia in the South Seas. Most people would have been shocked by the idea of a twenty-four-year-old woman taking such a trip, but the Meads were proud of her. She had been studying Polynesian culture, and this trip was a good way to get experience with her subject matter. Once there, she tried to blend in with native life, while at the same time she recorded her observations. Margaret spent almost a year in a village on the island of Tau, where she studied the lives of young girls between the ages of twelve and nineteen. Her findings became the subject of her best-selling book, *Coming of Age in Samoa*.

Margaret saw that to fully understand adolescents, she would need to study the lives of children, so she and Reo Fortune, a New Zealander also involved in anthropology, went to the island of New Guinea in the Pacific. She thought the best way of getting children to express themselves was through pictures that they drew. She brought along a thousand sheets of paper. They were gone in the first month! By the time Margaret left New Guinea, she had thirty-five thousand drawings. She had also become divorced from her husband, Luther Cressman, and had married Reo Fortune.

In each new place, Margaret tried to learn the language and understand the religion, moral values, and social lives of the people she studied. By doing this, she was developing a method of inquiry—observation, interviews, photographs—that other anthropologists could use. Her work required sensitivity and skill; Margaret had to talk to the right people, ask the right questions, and be astute enough to understand the unspoken answers that were revealed in the way people used their hands or head. All the photographs she took needed to be labeled with names and dates. Things she collected—jewelry, toys, utensils, tools, carvings, clothing—had to be identified and labeled as well.

Margaret continued her pioneering anthropological work for the next several decades. She went on trips back to New Guinea and to Bali as well, and she wrote more books that described what she had seen and learned. On Bali, Margaret met Gregory Bateson, an English anthropologist. Now divorced from Reo Fortune, Margaret married Gregory. In the late 1930s the threat of World War II kept her in America, where part of her time was spent working at the American Museum of Natural History in New York City. In 1939 she gave birth to a child of her own, Mary Catherine. After many years of studying children and teenagers, Margaret was now a mother herself.

As time passed, Margaret found the field trips—usually to countries where there was no running water or electricity—harder to make. She spent more time teaching anthropology at Columbia University. When she broke her ankle, she was bothered by crutches, so she got herself a slim cherry-wood stick with a Y-shaped fork at the top on which she could lean. Even after her ankle healed, she kept using the stick, and it became a kind of trademark, along with the bright red cape she always wore.

Margaret had come a long way from the little girl who made observations about her sisters. Her insights into the human family and its relationship to the world encouraged people to focus on the similarities they shared rather than the differences that divided them. She hoped that one day people might bring up children who were "able to be at home anywhere in the world, in any house, in any time band, eating any different kind of food, learning new languages as needed, never afraid of the new, sad to leave anywhere where one has been for a few days, but glad to go forward." Certainly, Margaret herself was always glad to take the next step.

TIME LINE

c. 1595	Pocahontas is born.
1607	English settlers establish a colony called Jamestown in what is now Virginia.
1614	Pocahontas is instructed in Christianity and baptized; marries John Rolfe.
1616	Pocahontas, John Rolfe, and their son, Thomas, set sail for England.
1617	Pocahontas dies.
1775	Revolutionary War begins.
1776	Congress publishes the Declaration of Independence.
1783	Treaty of Paris ends the Revolutionary War.
1815	Elizabeth Cady Stanton is born in Johnstown, New York.
1820	Susan B. Anthony is born in Adams, Massachusetts.
c. 1820	Harriet Tubman is born in Dorchester County, Maryland.
1821	Clara Barton is born in North Oxford, Massachusetts.
1827	Harriet Tubman is first "hired out" by her master.
1830	Emily Dickinson is born in Amherst, Massachusetts.
1834	Harriet Tubman helps a slave escape and receives the forehead wound that scars her for life.
1839	Clara Barton earns her teaching certificate and begins to teach school.
1844	Emily Dickinson's girlhood friend, Sophia Holland, dies. Emily is devastated and is sent to Boston to find new interests and distractions.
1844	Harriet and John Tubman marry.
1844	Mary Cassatt is born in Allegheny City, Pennsylvania.
1845	The Anthony family moves to Rochester, New York. Home becomes a meeting place for antislavery activists, including Frederick Douglass.
1847	Emily Dickinson attends Mount Holyoke Female Seminary.
1848	First Women's Rights Convention held in Seneca Falls, New York.
1849	Harriet Tubman escapes across the Mason-Dixon line to freedom.
1850	Susan B. Anthony and Elizabeth Cady Stanton meet for the first time.
1852	Clara Barton begins teaching in Bordentown, New Jersey, where she establishes a "free," or public, school.
1860	Abraham Lincoln is elected president.
1861	Civil War begins.
1861	Mary Cassatt begins to study painting at the Pennsylvania Academy of Fine Arts in Philadelphia.
1862	U.S. Surgeon General issues Clara Barton a military pass that allows her to nurse the wounded at the battlefront.
1863	Slavery is abolished.
1863	International Committee of the Red Cross is founded in Geneva, Switzerland.
1865	Civil War ends.
1865	After the war, Harriet Tubman returns to Auburn, New York, to care for her aging parents, Benjamin and Harriet.
1865	Abraham Lincoln is shot and killed by John Wilkes Booth.
1865	Clara Barton begins a national search for missing soldiers.
1866	Mary Cassatt leaves for Paris, France.
1868	Cassatt's first painting is accepted to the Paris Salon.
1869	Susan B. Anthony and Elizabeth Cady Stanton form the National Woman Suffrage Association; Stanton serves as its president for the next twenty-three years.
1869	Clara Barton sails to Europe and meets with representatives of the International Committee of the Red Cross.
1869	*Harriet Tubman: The Moses of Her People* is published; Harriet marries Nelson Davis.
1870–71	Clara Barton works with the International Red Cross during the Franco-Prussian War.
1880	Helen Keller is born in Tuscumbia, Alabama.
1881	United States establishes American Association of the Red Cross.
1884	Eleanor Roosevelt is born in New York City.
1884	Leaders of the International Red Cross amend the Treaty of Geneva to allow disaster relief.
1886	*Harriet Tubman, the Moses of Her People* is published, expanded from the original publication of 1869.

1886	Emily Dickinson dies.
1890	Emily Dickinson's poems are published posthumously.
1897	Amelia Earhart is born in Atchison, Kansas.
1898	Clara Barton helps victims of the Spanish-American War.
1901	Margaret Mead is born in Philadelphia, Pennsylvania.
1902	Elizabeth Cady Stanton dies.
1902	Helen Keller's autobiography, *The Story of My Life*, is published.
1904	Helen Keller graduates from Radcliffe College.
1904	Mary Cassatt is awarded France's Legion of Honor.
1905	Susan B. Anthony meets with President Theodore Roosevelt about suffrage amendment.
1905	Eleanor and Franklin D. Roosevelt marry.
1906	Susan B. Anthony dies.
1912	Clara Barton dies.
1913	Harriet Tubman dies.
1915	Helen Keller joins the National Women's Party.
1917	America enters World War I.
1920	United States passes the Nineteenth Amendment to the Constitution, granting women the right to vote.
1920	Cataracts and near blindness cause Mary Cassatt to stop painting.
1921	Amelia Earhart makes her first solo flight and receives her pilot's license.
1924	Helen Keller begins work for the American Foundation for the Blind.
1926	Mary Cassatt dies.
1926	Margaret Mead begins her tenure as assistant curator at the American Museum of Natural History in New York City.
1928	Amelia Earhart is the first woman to fly the Atlantic, accompanied by pilot Wilmer Stultz and mechanic Lou Gordon.
1928	Margaret Mead's *Coming of Age in Samoa* is published.
1929	Helen Keller's *Midstream: My Later Life* is published.
1929	Great Depression begins in America.
1931	Amelia Earhart marries publisher George Putnam.
1932	Amelia Earhart becomes the first woman to fly the Atlantic Ocean solo.
1932	Franklin Delano Roosevelt is elected president.
1935	Amelia Earhart makes the first solo flight from Hawaii to California.
1937	Amelia Earhart is lost at sea during a flight from New Guinea to Howland Island in the Pacific.
1937	Helen Keller tours Japan.
1941	America enters World War II.
1945	Franklin D. Roosevelt dies; Eleanor Roosevelt continues her humanitarian activities on a global scale, which earns her the title "First Lady of the World."
1945	World War II ends.
1946	Helen Keller visits Europe to raise money for the American Foundation for the Overseas Blind.
1948–52	Helen Keller makes further tours: to Australia, New Zealand, Japan, South Africa, and the Middle East.
1955	Rosa Parks, a black woman, refuses to give up her seat on a bus in Montgomery, Alabama; modern Civil Rights Movement is born.
1959	*The Miracle Worker*, a play and later a film, about Helen Keller and Annie Sullivan is first performed.
1960	John Fitzgerald Kennedy is elected president.
1962	Eleanor Roosevelt dies in New York City.
1963	More than 250,000 demonstrators march peacefully to the Lincoln Memorial in Washington, D.C., to pressure Congress to vote the Civil Rights bill into law; Martin Luther King, Jr. delivers his famous "I Have a Dream" speech to the crowd.
1963	John F. Kennedy is shot and killed by Lee Harvey Oswald.
1966	Susan B. Anthony House is designated a National Historic Landmark.
1968	Helen Keller dies.
1978	Margaret Mead dies.
1979	Margaret Mead is posthumously awarded the Presidential Medal of Freedom, the most prestigious civilian honor in the United States.

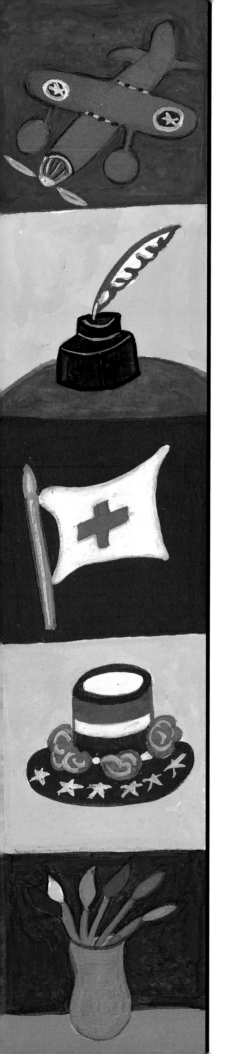

BIBLIOGRAPHY

Ashby, Ruth, and Deborah Gore Ohrn, eds. Herstory: *Women Who Changed the World.* New York: Viking, 1995.

Barton, Clara. *The Story of My Childhood.* New York: Arno Press, 1980.

Clinton, Susan. *The Story of Susan B. Anthony.* Chicago: The Children's Press, 1986.

Dolin, Arnold. *Great American Heroines.* New York: Hart Publishing Company, 1960.

Dubowski, Cathy East. *Clara Barton: Healing the Wounds.* Englewood Cliffs: Silver Burdett Press, 1991.

Faber, Doris, and Harold Faber. *American Government.* Great Lives series. New York: Atheneum Books for Young Readers, 1988.

Faber, Doris, and Harold Faber. *American Literature.* Great Lives series. New York: Atheneum Books for Young Readers, 1995.

Farr, Judith. *The Passion of Emily Dickinson.* Cambridge: Harvard University Press, 1992.

Fritz, Jean. *You Want Women to Vote, Lizzie Stanton?* New York: G. P. Putnam's Sons, 1995.

Garraty, John A., ed. *The Young People's Companion to American History.* Boston: Houghton Mifflin, 1994.

Graff, Stewart, and Polly Anne Graff. *Helen Keller, Crusader for the Blind and Deaf.* New York: Dell, 1991.

Hamilton, Leni. *Clara Barton.* New York: Chelsea House, 1988.

Herrmann, Dorothy. *Helen Keller: A Life.* New York: Alfred A. Knopf, 1998.

Hymowitz, Carol, and Michaele Weissman. *A History of Women in America.* New York: Bantam Books, 1978.

Jacobs, William Jay. *Human Rights.* Great Lives series. New York: Charles Scribner's Sons, 1990.

Johnson, Thomas B., ed. *Emily Dickinson: Selected Letters.* Cambridge: Harvard University Press, 1971.

Keller, Helen. *The Story of My Life.* New York: Signet, 1988.

Krull, Kathleen. *Lives of the Writers: Comedies, Tragedies, and What the Neighbors Thought.* San Diego: Harcourt Brace, 1994.

McMullan, Kate. *The Story of Harriet Tubman, Conductor of the Underground Railroad.* New York: Dell, 1991.

Mead, Margaret. *Blackberry Winter.* New York: William Morrow, 1972.

St. George, Judith. *Dear Dr. Bell . . . Your Friend, Helen Keller.* New York: Beech Tree Press, 1992.

Saunders, Susan. *Margaret Mead: The World Was Her Family.* New York: Puffin, 1987.

Sills, Leslie. *Visions: Stories About Women Artists.* Morton Grove, IL: Albert Whitman & Company, 1993.

Sloate, Susan. *Amelia Earhart: Challenging the Skies.* New York: Fawcett Columbine, 1990.

Sloate, Susan. *Clara Barton: Founder of the American Red Cross.* New York: Fawcett Columbine, 1990.

Sterling, Dorothy. *Freedom Train: The Story of Harriet Tubman.* New York: Scholastic Book Services, 1974.

Swain, Gwenyth. *The Road to Seneca Falls: A Story About Elizabeth Cady Stanton.* Minneapolis: Carolrhoda Books, 1996.

Taylor, M. W. *Harriet Tubman: Anti-Slavery Activist.* New York: Chelsea House, 1991.

Veglahn, Nancy. *Women Scientists.* New York: Facts on File, 1991.

Weisberg, Barbara. *Susan B. Anthony: Suffragist.* New York: Chelsea House, 1988.